The Industrial Revolution

American history, Volume 17

Michael Johnson

Published by Harmony House Publishing, 2024.

While every precaution has been taken in the preparation of this book, the publisher assumes no responsibility for errors or omissions, or for damages resulting from the use of the information contained herein.

THE INDUSTRIAL REVOLUTION

First edition. April 5, 2024.

Copyright © 2024 Michael Johnson.

ISBN: 979-8224699322

Written by Michael Johnson.

Table of Contents

"To the pioneers of progress and the architects of innovation,

This book is dedicated to the visionaries and trailblazers who propelled America into the age of industry. From the inventors who revolutionized technology to the laborers who toiled in factories, your ingenuity and perseverance laid the foundation for modern civilization. May your legacy inspire future generations to embrace change, pursue innovation, and forge a brighter tomorrow.

With gratitude and admiration,

Michael Johnson"

Chapter 1: Introduction to the Industrial Revolution

The Industrial Revolution stands as one of the most significant periods in human history, fundamentally transforming economies, societies, and lifestyles. Its impact reverberated across continents, reshaping the fabric of human existence and laying the groundwork for the modern world we inhabit today. This chapter delves into the essence of the Industrial Revolution, tracing its origins, exploring the historical context that propelled its emergence, and analyzing the key factors that fueled its unprecedented growth.

Definition and Overview

The Industrial Revolution refers to the profound socioeconomic transformation that occurred in the late 18th and early 19th centuries, primarily in Europe and North America. It marked a transition from agrarian and handicraft-based economies to mechanized manufacturing and industrial production. Central to this revolution was the adoption of new technologies, such as the steam engine, textile machinery, and iron production techniques, which revolutionized production processes, transportation, and communication.

At its core, the Industrial Revolution represents a shift from manual labor and decentralized production to mechanized factories and mass production. It led to increased urbanization as people migrated from rural areas to cities in search of employment opportunities in factories. This period witnessed unprecedented economic growth, but it also brought about significant social, environmental, and political changes, shaping the course of human history for centuries to come.

Historical Context Leading Up to the

Revolution

The seeds of the Industrial Revolution were sown centuries before its onset, as gradual changes in agriculture, trade, and technology laid the groundwork for a transformative shift in production methods. The medieval period saw the emergence of guilds and craft specialization, laying the foundation for early forms of manufacturing. The Renaissance and Scientific Revolution fostered intellectual curiosity and innovation, leading to groundbreaking discoveries in fields such as physics, chemistry, and engineering.

The Commercial Revolution of the 16th and 17th centuries fueled global trade and exploration, introducing new goods, technologies, and ideas to Europe. The colonization of the Americas and other regions provided access to vast reserves of natural resources, spurring economic growth and expanding markets. Concurrently, the enclosure movement in Britain consolidated land ownership, driving small farmers off the land and into wage labor.

The Enlightenment era ushered in an age of reason and skepticism, challenging traditional beliefs and institutions. Thinkers such as Adam Smith, with his seminal work "The Wealth of Nations," laid the intellectual groundwork for capitalism and free-market economics. The Enlightenment also fostered a spirit of inquiry and experimentation, paving the way for the scientific and technological advancements that would define the Industrial Revolution.

Key Factors Contributing to the Revolution

Several interrelated factors converged to catalyze the onset of the Industrial Revolution, each playing a crucial role in its development and spread.

1. Technological Innovation: Perhaps the most significant driver of the Industrial Revolution was the proliferation of new technologies that revolutionized production processes. Inventions such as the spinning

jenny, water frame, and power loom transformed the textile industry, increasing productivity and lowering costs. James Watt's steam engine, patented in 1769, powered factories, mines, and locomotives, providing a reliable source of mechanical power and enabling the mechanization of various industries.

2. Access to Natural Resources: The abundance of natural resources, particularly coal and iron ore, provided the raw materials necessary for industrialization. Britain, in particular, possessed vast coal reserves, which fueled steam engines and powered factories. The availability of iron ore facilitated the expansion of iron and steel production, essential for constructing machinery, railways, and infrastructure.

3. Capital Accumulation and Investment: The accumulation of capital through trade, colonialism, and agricultural innovations provided the financial resources needed to invest in industrial ventures. Merchant capitalists and entrepreneurs invested in factories, machinery, and infrastructure, driving technological innovation and economic growth. The emergence of joint-stock companies and stock exchanges facilitated the mobilization of capital on a scale never seen before, enabling large-scale industrial projects and investments.

4. Transportation and Communication: Improvements in transportation and communication networks facilitated the movement of goods, people, and information, accelerating economic exchange and industrial development. The construction of canals, such as the Bridgewater Canal in Britain, reduced the cost of transporting raw materials and finished goods, linking inland regions to coastal ports. The proliferation of railways, spurred by the invention of the steam locomotive, revolutionized long-distance transportation, enabling the rapid movement of goods and facilitating the growth of markets.

5. Urbanization and Labor Supply: The shift from rural agrarian lifestyles to urban industrial centers was a defining feature of the Industrial Revolution. Urbanization drew large numbers of people from the countryside to cities in search of employment in factories and mills.

The enclosure of common lands and displacement of small farmers pushed many into wage labor, while improvements in agricultural productivity reduced the need for labor in rural areas. The influx of rural migrants provided a ready supply of cheap labor for burgeoning industries, driving urban growth and industrial expansion.

6. Political and Legal Framework: Political stability, favorable legal frameworks, and supportive government policies played a crucial role in fostering industrialization. Countries such as Britain and the United States provided an environment conducive to entrepreneurship, innovation, and economic growth, with relatively low barriers to entry and limited government intervention in business affairs. Legal protections for property rights, patents, and contracts encouraged investment and innovation, providing incentives for individuals and companies to pursue industrial ventures.

In summary, the Industrial Revolution was a multifaceted phenomenon driven by technological innovation, access to resources, capital accumulation, improvements in transportation and communication, urbanization, and supportive political and legal frameworks. These factors combined to unleash a wave of economic and social change that reshaped the world in ways unimaginable to previous generations. In the chapters that follow, we will explore in greater detail the various dimensions of this transformative period and its enduring legacy on America's economy and society.

Chapter 2: Pre-Industrial America

Before the onset of the Industrial Revolution, America was predominantly a rural and agrarian society, characterized by subsistence farming, small-scale manufacturing, and a decentralized economy. This chapter provides an in-depth exploration of pre-industrial America, examining its economic and social structures, the significance of agriculture and cottage industries, and the technological advancements that laid the groundwork for the industrial transformation.

Overview of Pre-Industrial Economy and Society in America

Pre-industrial America was shaped by a combination of indigenous cultures and European colonization, with diverse economic activities and social structures varying across regions. Native American tribes practiced subsistence agriculture, hunting, and gathering, utilizing advanced agricultural techniques such as crop rotation, irrigation, and terracing. European settlers introduced new crops, livestock, and farming methods, gradually transforming the landscape and economy.

In the colonial period, agriculture formed the backbone of the economy, with most settlers engaged in farming to sustain their families and communities. Cash crops such as tobacco, rice, and indigo became significant exports, driving economic growth and trade with Europe. Small-scale manufacturing and craft production also thrived, with artisans producing goods such as textiles, pottery, and furniture for local consumption and export.

Socially, pre-industrial America was characterized by a hierarchical society, with distinctions based on wealth, landownership, and social status. Colonial society was stratified, with wealthy landowners, merchants, and planters at the top of the social hierarchy, followed by small farmers, artisans, laborers, and indentured servants. Slavery played a significant role in the southern colonies, where African slaves were exploited for labor on plantations producing cash crops.

Agricultural-Based Economy and Cottage Industries

Agriculture was the dominant economic activity in pre-industrial America, providing the foundation for subsistence and commercial livelihoods. The vast majority of settlers were farmers, cultivating crops such as corn, wheat, barley, oats, and potatoes for food, feed, and trade. Farming methods varied depending on geography, climate, and available resources, with distinct regional patterns emerging over time.

In New England and the Mid-Atlantic colonies, small family farms predominated, producing a diverse range of crops and livestock for local markets. Farming was labor-intensive, with families working their own land and relying on household labor for planting, harvesting, and processing crops. Subsistence farming was common, with surplus produce sold or traded for other goods.

In the southern colonies, plantation agriculture dominated the economy, with large-scale farms producing cash crops such as tobacco, rice, indigo, and later cotton. Plantations relied heavily on slave labor, with enslaved Africans forced to work long hours under harsh conditions to cultivate and harvest crops. The plantation system was highly profitable but also socially and economically exploitative, perpetuating racial inequality and dependence on slave labor.

Cottage industries emerged alongside agriculture, providing additional sources of income for rural households. Artisans and craftspeople produced goods such as textiles, pottery, tools, and household items in small workshops or home-based settings. Cottage industries played a vital role in supplementing farm incomes and meeting local demand for goods, particularly in regions with limited access to urban markets.

Technological Advancements Leading to the Revolution

While pre-industrial America was characterized by relatively simple and labor-intensive production methods, technological advancements laid the groundwork for the industrial transformation that would follow. Innovations in agriculture, manufacturing, and transportation gradually improved efficiency, productivity, and economic growth.

In agriculture, advancements such as the use of iron plows, seed drills, and crop rotation techniques improved yields and reduced labor requirements. Eli Whitney's invention of the cotton gin in 1793 revolutionized cotton production in the southern United States, dramatically increasing productivity and profitability. The cotton gin mechanized the process of separating cotton fibers from seeds, making cotton cultivation more profitable and fueling the expansion of slavery and the cotton economy.

In manufacturing, pre-industrial America relied primarily on hand tools and simple machinery for production. However, technological innovations such as the water wheel and windmill provided sources of mechanical power for mills and factories, enabling the mechanization of certain processes. Water-powered mills, for example, were used for grinding grain, sawing lumber, and processing textiles, increasing efficiency and output.

Transportation advancements also played a crucial role in pre-industrial America, facilitating trade, commerce, and communication. Rivers and coastal waterways served as primary arteries of transportation, with flatboats, keelboats, and sailing vessels carrying goods and passengers between inland settlements and coastal ports. Roads and trails were rudimentary, limiting overland travel and trade to local or regional networks.

In summary, pre-industrial America was characterized by an agrarian-based economy, cottage industries, and limited technological sophistication. Agriculture formed the backbone of the economy, with small family farms and plantation agriculture dominating rural life. Cottage industries provided additional sources of income, while technological advancements in agriculture, manufacturing, and transportation laid the foundation for the industrial revolution that would transform America's economy and society in the centuries to come.

Chapter 3: The Birth of Industry

The birth of industry in America marked a watershed moment in economic history, as the nation transitioned from agrarian-based economies to industrial powerhouses. This chapter delves into the early developments in industry and manufacturing in America, examining the rise of factories, mass production, and the transformative impact of inventions like the cotton gin and steam engine.

Early Developments in Industry and Manufacturing in America

The seeds of industrialization were sown in colonial America, as early settlers sought to replicate the manufacturing practices of their European counterparts. However, the vastness of the continent, coupled with a scarcity of skilled labor and capital, initially hindered the development of large-scale industry. Instead, small-scale artisanal production and household manufacturing predominated, with craftsmen producing goods such as textiles, pottery, and tools for local consumption.

Despite these challenges, several key industries emerged in colonial America, laying the groundwork for future industrial expansion. Shipbuilding, for example, flourished in coastal regions, with skilled craftsmen constructing vessels for trade, commerce, and maritime exploration. Ironworks and foundries produced iron and steel products for construction, tools, and machinery, utilizing local resources and labor.

The Industrial Revolution in America gained momentum in the early 19th century, fueled by a combination of technological innovation, capital investment, and favorable economic conditions. The War of 1812, for instance, disrupted trade with Europe, prompting American entrepreneurs to invest in domestic manufacturing to meet demand for goods previously imported from abroad. This period saw the establishment of early textile mills, ironworks, and machine shops, laying the foundation for industrial growth.

Rise of Factories and Mass Production

The rise of factories and mass production revolutionized the way goods were manufactured, leading to unprecedented levels of productivity, efficiency, and output. Factories emerged as centers of production, where workers operated specialized machinery in large-scale operations. This shift from decentralized, artisanal production to centralized factory production enabled economies of scale and the standardization of goods.

The textile industry played a pivotal role in driving industrialization in America, with the establishment of textile mills powered by waterwheels or steam engines. Francis Cabot Lowell's Waltham-Lowell system, introduced in the early 19th century, pioneered the integration of spinning and weaving processes under one roof, streamlining production and reducing costs. The Lowell Mills in Massachusetts became a model for factory-based textile production, employing thousands of workers and producing vast quantities of cloth for domestic and international markets.

In addition to textiles, other industries embraced factory-based production methods, including iron and steel manufacturing, shoemaking, and machinery production. The development of interchangeable parts, pioneered by Eli Whitney in the early 19th century, revolutionized manufacturing processes, enabling the mass production of standardized components for machinery, firearms, and other goods. This system of interchangeable parts laid the groundwork for modern assembly-line production techniques, streamlining production and reducing costs.

Impact of Inventions like the Cotton Gin and Steam Engine

Inventions such as the cotton gin and steam engine had a transformative impact on American industry and society, accelerating the pace of industrialization and shaping the course of economic development.

Eli Whitney's invention of the cotton gin in 1793 revolutionized cotton production in the southern United States, dramatically increasing productivity and profitability. The cotton gin mechanized the process of separating cotton fibers from seeds, making cotton cultivation more profitable and fueling the expansion of slavery and the cotton economy. The cotton gin spurred the growth of cotton plantations in the South, leading to increased demand for land, labor, and capital and reshaping regional economies and social structures.

The steam engine, invented by James Watt in the late 18th century, provided a reliable source of mechanical power that revolutionized industry, transportation, and communication. Steam-powered factories and mills replaced water-powered mills, enabling industrial production to expand beyond riverside locations and facilitating urbanization and economic growth. Steam-powered locomotives and steamships transformed transportation networks, connecting distant markets and accelerating the movement of goods, people, and ideas.

In summary, the birth of industry in America was characterized by the rise of factories, mass production, and the transformative impact of inventions such as the cotton gin and steam engine. These developments revolutionized manufacturing processes, accelerated economic growth, and reshaped American society, laying the foundation for the industrial powerhouse that would emerge in the years to come.

Chapter 4: Transportation Revolution

The transportation revolution stands as one of the most transformative aspects of the Industrial Revolution, reshaping economies, societies, and landscapes across the globe. This chapter explores the revolutionizing of transportation networks during the Industrial Revolution, focusing on the pivotal roles of canals, railroads, and steamships in connecting markets, facilitating trade, commerce, and urbanization.

Revolutionizing Transportation Networks

Prior to the transportation revolution, overland transportation relied primarily on rudimentary roads and trails, while waterways provided the most efficient means of long-distance transport. However, these methods were often slow, expensive, and limited in their capacity to connect distant markets. The transportation revolution brought about a paradigm shift, introducing new modes of transportation that revolutionized the movement of goods, people, and ideas.

Role of Canals

Canals played a central role in the transportation revolution, providing efficient and cost-effective means of inland water transport. Canals were artificial waterways constructed to connect rivers, lakes, and seas, enabling boats and barges to navigate inland regions and bypass natural obstacles such as rapids and waterfalls. In the United States, the Erie Canal, completed in 1825, was a landmark achievement in canal construction, connecting the Great Lakes to the Hudson River and opening up trade routes between the Atlantic seaboard and the interior of the country. The Erie Canal reduced transportation costs, facilitated the movement of goods and people, and spurred economic development along its route, leading to the growth of cities such as Buffalo, Rochester, and Syracuse.

Role of Railroads

Railroads emerged as the quintessential symbol of the transportation revolution, revolutionizing land-based transportation and facilitating the rapid expansion of markets and industries. Railroads offered several advantages over traditional modes of transport, including greater speed, reliability, and carrying capacity. The development of steam locomotives, powered by coal-fired boilers, enabled trains to travel at unprecedented speeds and haul heavy loads over long distances. The Baltimore and Ohio Railroad, chartered in 1827, was the first common carrier railroad in the United States, laying the foundation for the rapid expansion of rail networks across the country. Railroads played a crucial role in connecting urban centers, industrial hubs, and resource-rich regions, facilitating the movement of raw materials, finished goods, and people. Railroads also spurred urbanization, as cities grew along railroad lines, attracted by the opportunities for trade, commerce, and industry.

Role of Steamships

Steamships revolutionized maritime transportation, overcoming the limitations of wind and sail and enabling ships to travel faster, farther, and more reliably. Steam-powered vessels, equipped with steam engines fueled by coal, replaced sailing ships as the dominant mode of long-distance transport, connecting ports and continents in ways previously unimaginable. The development of paddlewheel and later screw propeller steamships transformed ocean travel, reducing voyage times and opening up new trade routes. The SS Great Western, launched in 1837, was one of the earliest successful steam-powered transatlantic passenger liners, heralding a new era of transoceanic travel and trade. Steamships facilitated the globalization of trade, linking distant markets and enabling the exchange of goods, ideas, and cultures. Steam-powered vessels also played a crucial role in the colonization of distant lands, as European powers used steamships to project their influence and control over overseas territories.

Impact on Trade, Commerce, and Urbanization

The transportation revolution had profound implications for trade, commerce, and urbanization, reshaping economic landscapes and social structures in profound ways. The development of efficient transportation networks reduced the cost and time of moving goods, facilitating trade and commerce on a scale never before seen. Markets expanded, as producers gained access to larger and more distant markets, while consumers enjoyed a wider variety of goods at lower prices. The transportation revolution also fueled urbanization, as cities grew along transportation routes, attracted by the opportunities for trade, commerce, and industry. Industrial centers such as Manchester, Birmingham, and Pittsburgh flourished, as factories and mills sprang up along canals, railroads, and rivers, harnessing the power of transportation to drive economic growth and innovation.

In summary, the transportation revolution was a defining aspect of the Industrial Revolution, transforming the movement of goods, people, and ideas and reshaping economic landscapes and social structures. Canals, railroads, and steamships revolutionized transportation networks, connecting markets, facilitating trade, commerce, and urbanization, and laying the foundation for the globalized world we inhabit today.

Chapter 5: Urbanization and Migration

Urbanization and migration were pivotal aspects of the Industrial Revolution, as millions of people moved from rural areas to burgeoning urban centers in search of employment, opportunity, and a better life. This chapter explores the growth of cities and urban centers, the factors driving migration from rural to urban areas, and the social and demographic changes resulting from urbanization.

Growth of Cities and Urban Centers

The Industrial Revolution sparked a wave of urbanization as people flocked to cities and urban centers in search of employment in factories, mills, and industries. Cities became hubs of industry, commerce, and innovation, attracting people from rural areas and overseas with the promise of economic opportunity and social mobility. The growth of cities was fueled by several factors, including technological advancements, changes in agricultural practices, and demographic shifts.

Technological advancements such as the steam engine, mechanized production, and transportation networks facilitated the concentration of industry and commerce in urban areas. Factories, mills, and workshops sprang up in cities, powered by steam engines and connected to markets by canals, railroads, and steamships. Urban centers became centers of innovation and entrepreneurship, attracting skilled workers, engineers, and inventors seeking to capitalize on the opportunities afforded by industrialization.

Changes in agricultural practices also contributed to the growth of cities, as improvements in farming techniques and mechanization reduced the need for labor in rural areas. The enclosure movement, which consolidated land ownership and displaced small farmers, pushed many rural residents off the land and into wage labor, forcing them to seek employment in urban industries. Population growth and demographic changes further fueled urbanization, as people migrated from rural areas to cities in search of better economic prospects and improved living standards.

Migration from Rural Areas to Urban Areas

Migration from rural areas to urban areas was a defining feature of the Industrial Revolution, as millions of people left the countryside behind in search of employment and opportunity in cities. Rural residents were drawn to cities by the promise of steady wages, access to markets and services, and the allure of urban amenities such as theaters, shops, and cultural institutions. The lure of urban life, combined with the push factors of rural poverty, landlessness, and agricultural decline, spurred mass migration to urban centers.

The process of urban migration was often arduous and fraught with challenges, as migrants faced overcrowded living conditions, poor sanitation, and inadequate housing in the rapidly growing cities. Many migrants lived in cramped tenements and slums, lacking access to clean water, sanitation facilities, and basic amenities. Urbanization also brought social and cultural upheaval, as migrants from diverse backgrounds and regions came together in the melting pot of the city, bringing with them their customs, traditions, and languages.

Social and Demographic Changes Resulting from Urbanization

Urbanization brought about significant social and demographic changes, transforming the fabric of society and reshaping the lives of individuals and communities. Cities became melting pots of diversity, as people from different regions, ethnicities, and social classes came together in pursuit of economic opportunity. The mixing of diverse populations led to the emergence of new social and cultural identities, as urban residents forged new ways of living, working, and interacting with one another.

The growth of cities also led to changes in family structure and social relationships, as traditional kinship networks and rural communities gave way to urban anonymity and individualism. Extended families were replaced by nuclear families living in close quarters, as people sought to adapt to the demands of urban life. Women entered the workforce in greater numbers, working in factories, mills, and domestic service to supplement family incomes and contribute to the household economy.

Urbanization also brought about changes in political and economic structures, as cities became centers of political power and economic influence. Urban elites, including industrialists, merchants, and financiers, wielded significant political and economic clout, shaping government policies and investment priorities to suit their interests. Working-class movements emerged in response to the challenges of urban life, advocating for labor rights, social reforms, and improved living conditions for urban residents.

In summary, urbanization and migration were transformative aspects of the Industrial Revolution, reshaping economies, societies, and landscapes in profound ways. The growth of cities and urban centers, driven by technological advancements, changes in agricultural practices, and demographic shifts, brought about significant social and demographic changes, as people migrated from rural areas to urban centers in search of employment, opportunity, and a better life. Urbanization transformed the fabric of society, leading to the emergence of new social and cultural identities, family structures, and political and economic structures that continue to shape the world we inhabit today.

Chapter 6: Labor and Working Conditions

The rise of the industrial workforce during the Industrial Revolution brought about profound changes in the nature of work and employment. This chapter delves into the conditions faced by workers in factories and mines, the emergence of labor movements, and the early attempts at organizing for workers' rights.

Rise of the Industrial Workforce

The Industrial Revolution saw the transformation of work from decentralized, artisanal production to centralized factory-based manufacturing. As industries expanded and technology advanced, a new class of industrial workers emerged, drawn from rural areas and displaced from traditional agricultural livelihoods. These workers, including men, women, and children, formed the backbone of industrial production, operating machinery, tending to looms, and performing manual labor in factories and mines.

Workers in factories and mines faced grueling hours, low wages, and hazardous working conditions, as industrial capitalism prioritized profit over the well-being of employees. Many workers lived in poverty, struggling to make ends meet on meager wages and facing harsh penalties for absenteeism or insubordination. Children as young as six or seven were often employed in factories and mines, working long hours in dangerous conditions for little pay.

Working Conditions in Factories and Mines

Working conditions in factories and mines during the Industrial Revolution were notoriously harsh and dangerous, with little regard for the health and safety of workers. Factories were often crowded and poorly ventilated, with machines running at breakneck speed and workers packed tightly together on factory floors. Machinery lacked safety guards, exposing workers to the risk of injury and death from accidents and industrial hazards.

In textile mills, workers toiled for twelve to sixteen hours a day, six days a week, operating machines and performing repetitive tasks in noisy and dusty environments. Women and children made up a significant portion of the factory workforce, often working alongside men in physically demanding jobs. In coal mines, workers labored in cramped and poorly ventilated conditions, extracting coal from underground shafts and facing the constant threat of cave-ins, explosions, and accidents.

Child labor was widespread in factories and mines, as employers sought to maximize profits by employing cheap and easily exploitable labor. Children as young as six or seven were employed in textile mills, coal mines, and other industries, working long hours for minimal pay and enduring harsh treatment from supervisors. Child labor laws were virtually nonexistent, and efforts to regulate or restrict the employment of children were met with resistance from industrialists and employers.

Labor Movements and Early Attempts at Organizing for Workers' Rights

Despite the harsh working conditions and exploitation faced by industrial workers, resistance and organized efforts to improve labor conditions began to emerge during the Industrial Revolution. Workers formed mutual aid societies, trade unions, and cooperative societies to provide support, solidarity, and advocacy for their members. These early labor movements laid the groundwork for the organized labor movement that would emerge in the 19th and 20th centuries.

One of the earliest labor organizations was the Grand National Consolidated Trades Union (GNCTU), founded in Britain in 1834, which sought to unite workers across different trades and industries to demand better wages, hours, and working conditions. Although short-lived, the GNCTU inspired subsequent labor movements and demonstrated the potential power of collective action in confronting industrial capitalism.

In the United States, labor organizations such as the Knights of Labor and the American Federation of Labor (AFL) emerged in the late 19th century, advocating for the rights of industrial workers and engaging in strikes, boycotts, and other forms of collective action to press for better wages and working conditions. The Haymarket affair of 1886, in which a labor rally in Chicago turned violent, galvanized public support for the labor movement and led to widespread recognition of May Day as International Workers' Day.

Efforts to improve working conditions and protect workers' rights also led to the passage of legislation aimed at regulating industrial labor and promoting social welfare. In Britain, the Factory Acts of the 19th century imposed restrictions on child labor, limited working hours, and improved safety standards in factories and mines. Similar legislation was enacted in other countries, including the United States, where progressive reformers advocated for laws to protect workers and promote social justice.

In summary, the risc of the industrial workforce during the Industrial Revolution brought about profound changes in the nature of work and employment. Workers in factories and mines faced grueling hours, low wages, and hazardous working conditions, leading to the emergence of labor movements and early attempts at organizing for workers' rights. Despite the challenges faced by industrial workers, their struggles and activism laid the groundwork for the labor movement that would emerge in the following centuries, leading to significant improvements in working conditions, wages, and social welfare.

Chapter 7: Technological Innovations

The Industrial Revolution was characterized by a wave of technological innovations that revolutionized production processes, transportation, communication, and daily life. This chapter explores the key technological innovations of the Industrial Revolution, their impact on productivity, efficiency, and quality of life, and the contributions of inventors and entrepreneurs to industrial development.

Key Technological Innovations of the Industrial Revolution

1. Steam Engine: The steam engine, invented by Thomas Newcomen in 1712 and improved upon by James Watt in 1769, was one of the most transformative inventions of the Industrial Revolution. Steam engines provided a reliable source of mechanical power, driving machinery in factories, powering locomotives and steamships, and facilitating the mechanization of various industries.

2. Textile Machinery: The mechanization of textile production revolutionized the textile industry, leading to the development of spinning and weaving machinery that increased productivity and lowered costs. Inventions such as the spinning jenny, water frame, and power loom enabled the mass production of textiles, fueling the growth of the textile industry and providing affordable clothing for the masses.

3. Iron and Steel Production: Advances in iron and steel production techniques, including the use of coke instead of charcoal and improvements in blast furnace design, led to a dramatic increase in the production of iron and steel. The Bessemer process, developed by Henry Bessemer in the 1850s, further revolutionized steelmaking by enabling the production of large quantities of high-quality steel at lower cost.

4. Transportation Technologies: Transportation technologies such as canals, railroads, and steamships played a crucial role in connecting

markets, facilitating trade, and accelerating economic growth. The construction of canals such as the Erie Canal in the United States and the Bridgewater Canal in Britain enabled the efficient movement of goods and raw materials, while the development of steam-powered locomotives and steamships revolutionized long-distance transportation.

5. Communication Technologies: Communication technologies such as the telegraph and the printing press transformed the way information was disseminated, enabling rapid communication over long distances and facilitating the spread of ideas and knowledge. The invention of the telegraph by Samuel Morse in the 1830s revolutionized communication by allowing messages to be transmitted electronically over telegraph wires, paving the way for the development of global communication networks.

Impact of Inventions on Productivity, Efficiency, and Quality of Life

The technological innovations of the Industrial Revolution had a profound impact on productivity, efficiency, and quality of life, transforming economies, societies, and daily life in ways previously unimaginable.

1. Increased Productivity: The adoption of machinery and mechanized production processes led to a dramatic increase in productivity, allowing goods to be produced more quickly and at lower cost. This increase in productivity fueled economic growth and enabled the mass production of goods, leading to higher standards of living for many people.

2. Improved Efficiency: Technological innovations improved efficiency by streamlining production processes, reducing waste, and increasing output. For example, the introduction of the assembly line by Henry Ford in the early 20th century revolutionized manufacturing by

allowing products to be assembled more quickly and efficiently, leading to lower costs and increased production volumes.

3. Enhanced Quality of Life: The technological innovations of the Industrial Revolution led to improvements in living standards and quality of life for many people. Advances in transportation and communication made it easier for people to travel and communicate over long distances, while improvements in healthcare and sanitation led to reductions in disease and mortality rates.

Contributions of Inventors and Entrepreneurs to Industrial Development

The Industrial Revolution was driven by the ingenuity and entrepreneurial spirit of inventors and entrepreneurs who developed and commercialized new technologies, processes, and products.

1. James Watt: James Watt's improvements to the steam engine revolutionized industry and transportation, providing a reliable source of mechanical power that drove machinery in factories and powered locomotives and steamships.

2. Richard Arkwright: Richard Arkwright's invention of the water frame and the spinning frame revolutionized the textile industry by enabling the mass production of yarn and cloth, leading to the growth of textile factories and the expansion of the textile industry.

3. Henry Bessemer: Henry Bessemer's development of the Bessemer process revolutionized steelmaking by enabling the production of large quantities of high-quality steel at lower cost, leading to the widespread use of steel in construction, transportation, and industry.

4. Samuel Morse: Samuel Morse's invention of the telegraph revolutionized communication by allowing messages to be transmitted electronically over telegraph wires, paving the way for the development of global communication networks and the modern telecommunications industry.

5. Henry Ford: Henry Ford's introduction of the assembly line revolutionized manufacturing by allowing products to be assembled more quickly and efficiently, leading to lower costs and increased production volumes.

In summary, the technological innovations of the Industrial Revolution revolutionized production processes, transportation, communication, and daily life, transforming economies, societies, and living standards. The contributions of inventors and entrepreneurs played a crucial role in driving industrial development and shaping the world we inhabit today.

Chapter 8: Economic Transformation

The Industrial Revolution marked a profound shift in economic paradigms, transforming societies from agrarian-based economies to industrial powerhouses. This chapter explores the shift from agrarian to industrial economies, the growth of domestic and international markets, and the rise of capitalism and modern business practices.

Shift from Agrarian to Industrial Economy

The Industrial Revolution heralded a seismic shift in economic structures, as societies transitioned from predominantly agrarian economies to industrial economies. Prior to the Industrial Revolution, the majority of people were engaged in agricultural activities, cultivating crops, and raising livestock to sustain themselves and their communities. However, the advent of mechanized production and technological innovations transformed the way goods were produced, leading to the rise of factory-based manufacturing and the mass production of goods.

The mechanization of agriculture also played a crucial role in the shift from agrarian to industrial economies, as advancements such as the seed drill, mechanical reaper, and threshing machine increased agricultural productivity and reduced the need for manual labor. As a result, fewer people were required to work in agriculture, freeing up labor for employment in factories, mines, and industries.

Growth of Domestic and International Markets

The Industrial Revolution fueled the growth of domestic and international markets, as factories churned out goods at unprecedented rates and transportation networks expanded to connect distant markets. Mass production techniques enabled the production of goods on a scale never before seen, leading to a proliferation of consumer goods and an increase in consumer demand.

The development of transportation technologies such as canals, railroads, and steamships facilitated the movement of goods and people over long distances, enabling the efficient exchange of goods between regions and nations. Canals such as the Erie Canal in the United States and the Manchester Ship Canal in Britain provided vital links between inland manufacturing centers and coastal ports, while railroads crisscrossed continents, connecting cities and industrial hubs.

The growth of international trade and commerce also played a significant role in the economic transformation of the Industrial Revolution, as nations exchanged goods and resources in a global marketplace. European powers established colonial empires in Africa, Asia, and the Americas, exploiting the natural resources and labor of colonized peoples to fuel their industrial economies. Raw materials such as cotton, rubber, and coal were extracted from colonies and shipped back to Europe to be processed and manufactured into finished goods.

Rise of Capitalism and Emergence of Modern Business Practices

The Industrial Revolution saw the rise of capitalism as the dominant economic system, characterized by private ownership of the means of production, free markets, and the pursuit of profit. Entrepreneurs and industrialists capitalized on technological innovations and market opportunities to build vast industrial empires, amassing wealth and power in the process.

The emergence of modern business practices such as corporate organization, finance, and management played a crucial role in the economic transformation of the Industrial Revolution. Joint-stock companies and corporations enabled investors to pool their resources and spread risk, facilitating the large-scale investment needed to finance industrial projects such as factories, mines, and railroads.

In addition, innovations in finance and banking, such as the establishment of central banks and the development of stock exchanges, provided the capital and liquidity needed to fuel economic growth and expansion. Financial instruments such as stocks, bonds, and credit facilitated investment and capital formation, enabling entrepreneurs to finance new ventures and expand their businesses.

The rise of capitalism also led to significant social and economic changes, as wealth became concentrated in the hands of a small elite while workers faced exploitation and inequality. The growth of industrial capitalism fueled the rise of class conflict and labor movements, as workers organized to demand better wages, working conditions, and rights.

In summary, the Industrial Revolution brought about a profound economic transformation, shifting societies from agrarian to industrial economies and fueling the growth of domestic and international markets. The rise of capitalism and the emergence of modern business practices revolutionized economic structures and systems, shaping the world we inhabit today.

Chapter 9: Social Impact and Change

The Industrial Revolution brought about profound social transformations, reshaping existing social structures and hierarchies, redefining family life and gender roles, and presenting both challenges and opportunities for different social classes. This chapter explores the social impact and change wrought by the Industrial Revolution, examining its effects on social structures, family dynamics, gender roles, and social mobility.

Transformation of Social Structures and Hierarchies

The Industrial Revolution brought about a fundamental transformation of social structures and hierarchies, as traditional agrarian societies gave way to industrial urban centers. In rural areas, where the majority of the population had previously been engaged in agriculture, the rise of mechanized farming and the consolidation of land ownership led to the displacement of small farmers and the concentration of land in the hands of wealthy landowners. This shift exacerbated social inequalities and contributed to the emergence of a rural proletariat, comprising landless laborers and tenant farmers who worked for wages on large estates.

In urban areas, the growth of factories and industries fueled the rise of a new industrial working class, composed of men, women, and children who labored in factories, mills, and mines. Factory work was often grueling and dangerous, with long hours, low wages, and harsh working conditions. The industrial working class lived in crowded tenements and slums, lacking access to clean water, sanitation, and basic amenities. Despite these challenges, urbanization also provided opportunities for social mobility, as people migrated from rural areas to cities in search of employment and opportunity.

Impact on Family Life, Gender Roles, and Social Mobility

The Industrial Revolution had a profound impact on family life, reshaping family dynamics, and altering traditional gender roles. In agrarian societies, families were often self-sufficient units, with household members working together on the family farm or in cottage industries to produce goods for their own consumption. However, the rise of factory-based production and the separation of work from the home led to a division of labor along gender lines, with men working outside the home in factories and mines while women and children remained at home to care for the household and children.

The separation of work from the home also had significant implications for family life, as families became increasingly fragmented and dislocated. Men, women, and children spent long hours apart, working in factories and mills, and often faced harsh conditions and exploitation. Children as young as six or seven were employed in factories and mines, working long hours for minimal pay and enduring dangerous working conditions.

The Industrial Revolution also presented opportunities for social mobility, as people from rural areas and lower social classes migrated to cities in search of employment and opportunity. The growth of industries and the expansion of urban centers created new avenues for advancement, enabling individuals to rise above their social origins through hard work, entrepreneurship, and innovation. However, social mobility was often limited by factors such as gender, race, and class, with opportunities for advancement disproportionately available to privileged groups.

Challenges and Opportunities for Different Social Classes

The Industrial Revolution presented both challenges and opportunities for different social classes, reshaping the social landscape and creating new opportunities for some while exacerbating inequalities for others. The rise of industrial capitalism led to the concentration of wealth and power in the hands of a small elite, as industrialists and entrepreneurs amassed vast fortunes through the exploitation of labor and the accumulation of capital.

For the working class, the Industrial Revolution brought about significant challenges, as men, women, and children toiled in factories and mines for meager wages and endured harsh working conditions. Factory work was often dangerous and exploitative, with little regard for the health and safety of workers. However, the growth of industries and the expansion of urban centers also provided opportunities for social mobility, enabling individuals to improve their economic prospects and social status through hard work and perseverance.

For the middle class, the Industrial Revolution brought about new opportunities for entrepreneurship and innovation, as individuals seized upon the possibilities afforded by technological advancements and market opportunities to build successful businesses and enterprises. The rise of capitalism and the emergence of modern business practices created new avenues for wealth creation and social advancement, enabling individuals to rise above their social origins and achieve success through their own efforts.

In summary, the Industrial Revolution brought about profound social transformations, reshaping existing social structures and hierarchies, redefining family life and gender roles, and presenting both challenges and opportunities for different social classes. The rise of industrial capitalism and the emergence of modern business practices created new opportunities for entrepreneurship and innovation, while also exacerbating inequalities and exploitation for the working class.

Despite these challenges, the Industrial Revolution laid the groundwork for the modern world we inhabit today, shaping economies, societies, and cultures in profound and lasting ways.

Chapter 10: Environmental Impact

The Industrial Revolution brought about unprecedented economic growth and technological advancements, but it also had profound environmental consequences. This chapter explores the environmental impact of industrialization, including pollution, deforestation, and resource depletion, as well as early awareness of environmental issues and efforts at conservation.

Environmental Consequences of Industrialization

1. Pollution: Industrialization led to widespread pollution of air, water, and soil as factories, mills, and mines released pollutants into the environment. Smokestack emissions from coal-fired factories and steam engines polluted the air with sulfur dioxide, particulate matter, and other harmful substances, leading to respiratory problems, acid rain, and smog. Water pollution was also rampant, as industrial effluents contaminated rivers, streams, and waterways with heavy metals, chemicals, and toxins, posing risks to aquatic ecosystems and public health. Soil pollution resulted from industrial waste disposal and chemical runoff from agricultural fields, degrading soil quality and reducing fertility.

2. Deforestation: The demand for timber, fuel, and land for agriculture led to widespread deforestation during the Industrial Revolution. Forests were cleared to make way for farms, factories, and urban development, leading to habitat loss, biodiversity decline, and soil erosion. Deforestation also contributed to climate change by reducing the capacity of forests to absorb carbon dioxide and regulate the Earth's climate.

3. Resource Depletion: The Industrial Revolution accelerated the exploitation and depletion of natural resources such as coal, oil, and minerals. The demand for coal as a fuel for steam engines and industrial

processes led to the widespread extraction of coal reserves, resulting in environmental degradation, habitat destruction, and landscape alteration. Similarly, the extraction of oil and minerals for use in industry and manufacturing contributed to habitat destruction, pollution, and resource depletion.

Early Awareness of Environmental Issues and Efforts at Conservation

1. Conservation Movements: Despite the widespread environmental degradation caused by industrialization, early awareness of environmental issues and efforts at conservation began to emerge during the Industrial Revolution. Conservation movements such as the establishment of national parks and nature reserves sought to protect natural landscapes and biodiversity from the impacts of industrial development. For example, the creation of Yellowstone National Park in the United States in 1872 marked the beginning of the national park movement, which aimed to preserve pristine wilderness areas for future generations.

2. Environmental Legislation: Governments began to recognize the need for environmental regulation and legislation to address the environmental consequences of industrialization. In the United States, the establishment of the Environmental Protection Agency (EPA) in 1970 marked a milestone in environmental policy, as the agency was tasked with regulating pollution, enforcing environmental laws, and protecting public health and the environment. Similarly, the passage of environmental laws such as the Clean Air Act, Clean Water Act, and Endangered Species Act provided legal frameworks for addressing environmental issues and protecting natural resources.

3. Technological Innovations: Technological innovations played a crucial role in mitigating the environmental impacts of industrialization and advancing conservation efforts. For example, the development of

pollution control technologies such as scrubbers, catalytic converters, and wastewater treatment systems helped reduce emissions and mitigate pollution from industrial sources. Similarly, advancements in renewable energy technologies such as solar, wind, and hydroelectric power offered alternatives to fossil fuels and contributed to efforts to combat climate change and promote sustainability.

4. Environmental Awareness: The Industrial Revolution also fostered a growing awareness of environmental issues and the need for sustainable development. Environmental organizations, advocacy groups, and grassroots movements emerged to raise awareness, promote conservation, and mobilize public support for environmental protection. For example, the Sierra Club, founded in 1892, became a leading voice for conservation and environmental activism, advocating for the protection of wilderness areas, national parks, and endangered species.

In summary, the Industrial Revolution had profound environmental consequences, including pollution, deforestation, and resource depletion. However, it also led to early awareness of environmental issues and efforts at conservation, including the establishment of national parks, environmental legislation, technological innovations, and environmental awareness campaigns. While the environmental legacy of the Industrial Revolution remains a challenge to address, these early efforts laid the groundwork for modern environmental conservation and sustainability initiatives.

Chapter 11: Cultural Shifts

The Industrial Revolution brought about profound cultural shifts, reshaping society's values, norms, and creative expressions. This chapter explores the changes in culture, arts, and literature during the Industrial Revolution, the impact of urbanization and technological advancements on society, and the responses to modernity and industrialization in popular culture.

Changes in Culture, Arts, and Literature

1. Urbanization and Industrialization: The rapid urbanization and industrialization of the Industrial Revolution had a transformative impact on culture, arts, and literature. As people migrated from rural areas to cities in search of employment and opportunity, urban centers became vibrant hubs of creativity, innovation, and cultural exchange. The growth of industries, factories, and workshops provided opportunities for artists, writers, and intellectuals to engage with new ideas, technologies, and social movements.

2. Shift in Values and Ideals: The Industrial Revolution brought about a shift in values and ideals, as traditional agrarian societies gave way to modern urban centers. The pursuit of progress, innovation, and economic growth became central to the cultural ethos of the time, as society embraced the ideals of industrial capitalism and technological advancement. However, this emphasis on materialism and consumerism also led to critiques of the social and environmental costs of industrialization, as artists and writers grappled with the human consequences of rapid technological change.

3. Response to Social Change: The cultural responses to social change during the Industrial Revolution were diverse and varied, reflecting the complexities and contradictions of the time. Some artists and writers embraced the spirit of progress and modernity, celebrating

the achievements of industrialization and urbanization in their work. Others, however, were critical of the social inequalities and injustices brought about by industrial capitalism, using their art and literature to advocate for social reform and political change.

Impact of Urbanization and Technological Advancements on Society

1. Urban Culture and Lifestyle: The rise of urbanization and technological advancements transformed society's culture and lifestyle, as people adapted to the rhythms and realities of urban life. Urban centers became melting pots of diversity, as people from different backgrounds and regions came together in the bustling streets and neighborhoods of the city. The growth of industries and the expansion of transportation networks also led to changes in leisure activities and social interactions, as people had more leisure time and disposable income to spend on entertainment, recreation, and consumer goods.

2. Technological Innovations in the Arts: The Industrial Revolution spurred technological innovations in the arts, enabling new forms of creative expression and communication. The invention of photography, for example, revolutionized visual culture by allowing artists to capture and reproduce images with unprecedented precision and detail. Similarly, advancements in printing technology led to the proliferation of newspapers, magazines, and books, democratizing access to information and ideas and shaping public discourse on social and political issues.

3. Transformation of Public Spaces: The transformation of public spaces during the Industrial Revolution reflected the changing social and cultural dynamics of the time. Urban centers were redesigned and reimagined to accommodate the needs of a growing population, with the construction of parks, gardens, and public squares providing spaces for recreation, relaxation, and social interaction. The rise of consumer

culture also led to the proliferation of commercial establishments such as theaters, cafes, and department stores, which became hubs of social life and cultural exchange.

Responses to Modernity and Industrialization in Popular Culture

1. Literature and Fiction: Literature and fiction played a crucial role in reflecting and shaping society's responses to modernity and industrialization during the Industrial Revolution. Writers such as Charles Dickens, Elizabeth Gaskell, and Thomas Hardy explored the human consequences of rapid social and economic change in their novels, depicting the struggles of working-class individuals and families against the backdrop of industrial capitalism and urbanization. These works often critiqued the social inequalities and injustices of the time while advocating for empathy, compassion, and social reform.

2. Visual Arts and Painting: Visual arts and painting also responded to the cultural shifts and technological advancements of the Industrial Revolution, capturing the changing landscapes and social dynamics of the time. Artists such as J.M.W. Turner and John Constable depicted the effects of industrialization and urbanization on the natural environment, portraying scenes of industrial landscapes, polluted rivers, and smog-filled skies. These works served as powerful critiques of the environmental and social costs of industrialization, urging viewers to consider the human impact of technological progress and economic growth.

3. Music and Performing Arts: Music and performing arts reflected the diversity and dynamism of urban culture during the Industrial Revolution, incorporating elements of folk, classical, and popular music into new forms of entertainment and expression. The rise of music halls, theaters, and concert venues provided platforms for artists and performers to showcase their talents and connect with audiences from

diverse backgrounds and social classes. Similarly, the development of new musical instruments and technologies expanded the possibilities for musical composition and performance, leading to the emergence of new genres and styles that reflected the spirit of the times.

In summary, the Industrial Revolution brought about profound cultural shifts, reshaping society's values, norms, and creative expressions. The changes in culture, arts, and literature during this period reflected the impact of urbanization and technological advancements on society, as well as the responses to modernity and industrialization in popular culture. Despite the challenges and contradictions of the time, the cultural legacy of the Industrial Revolution continues to shape the world we inhabit today, influencing our values, beliefs, and artistic expressions.

Chapter 12: Economic Expansion and Global Influence

The Industrial Revolution propelled the United States into a period of unprecedented economic expansion and global influence. This chapter explores the expansion of American industry and influence beyond national borders, the role of American exports in global trade networks, and the impact on geopolitics and international relations.

Expansion of American Industry and Influence Beyond National Borders

1. Industrial Growth: The Industrial Revolution transformed the United States into an industrial powerhouse, as factories, mills, and workshops sprung up across the country, churning out goods for domestic and international markets. The expansion of industries such as textiles, steel, and machinery fueled economic growth and prosperity, attracting investment, entrepreneurs, and skilled workers from around the world.

2. Technological Advancements: Technological advancements played a crucial role in driving industrial growth and expansion, as innovations such as the steam engine, telegraph, and railroad revolutionized transportation, communication, and production processes. The development of new technologies and manufacturing techniques enabled American industries to increase productivity, lower costs, and compete more effectively in global markets.

3. Infrastructure Development: Infrastructure development was critical to the expansion of American industry and influence beyond national borders, as investments in transportation, communication, and energy infrastructure facilitated the movement of goods, people, and capital. The construction of canals, railroads, and steamships connected distant markets and opened up new trade routes, while the expansion of

telegraph lines and communication networks facilitated the exchange of information and ideas.

Role of American Exports in Global Trade Networks

1. Export-Led Growth: American exports played a crucial role in driving economic growth and development during the Industrial Revolution, as the United States emerged as a leading exporter of agricultural products, raw materials, and manufactured goods. The abundance of natural resources such as cotton, coal, and iron ore, combined with technological advancements and entrepreneurial ingenuity, enabled American industries to produce goods of high quality and competitive prices for export to global markets.

2. Expansion of Trade Networks: The expansion of American industry and influence led to the creation of extensive trade networks that connected the United States to markets around the world. American merchants and traders established commercial ties with Europe, Asia, and Latin America, exchanging goods, capital, and ideas in a global marketplace. The growth of international trade fostered economic interdependence and cultural exchange, shaping the course of globalization and international relations.

3. Impact on Global Economy: American exports had a significant impact on the global economy, contributing to the growth and prosperity of trading partners and fueling economic development in regions around the world. The export of agricultural products such as cotton, tobacco, and grain helped meet the growing demand for food and raw materials in Europe and other markets, while the export of manufactured goods such as textiles, machinery, and steel provided essential inputs for industrialization and modernization.

Impact on Geopolitics and International

Relations

1. Rise of American Hegemony: The expansion of American industry and influence during the Industrial Revolution transformed the United States into a global superpower, reshaping the balance of power and influence in international relations. American economic strength and military power enabled the United States to assert its interests and influence on the world stage, shaping the course of geopolitics and international affairs.

2. Competition and Conflict: The rise of American hegemony sparked competition and conflict with other global powers, as nations vied for control over strategic resources, markets, and territories. Economic rivalries and geopolitical tensions fueled conflicts such as the Opium Wars, the Scramble for Africa, and the Great Game, as competing powers sought to expand their spheres of influence and secure their interests in a changing world order.

3. Diplomacy and Alliances: American economic expansion and global influence also shaped the course of diplomacy and alliances, as the United States sought to promote its interests and values through diplomatic engagement and coalition-building. The expansion of American trade and investment abroad led to the negotiation of trade agreements, treaties, and alliances with other nations, establishing frameworks for cooperation and collaboration in areas such as commerce, security, and governance.

In summary, the Industrial Revolution propelled the United States into a period of unprecedented economic expansion and global influence, as American industry and exports transformed the country into a global superpower. The expansion of American industry and influence beyond national borders reshaped global trade networks, geopolitics, and international relations, leaving a lasting legacy that continues to shape the world we inhabit today.

Chapter 13: Resistance and Reform

The Industrial Revolution brought about unprecedented economic growth and technological advancements, but it also led to profound social and economic upheaval. This chapter explores the challenges to industrialization and responses from various groups, including labor strikes, protests, and movements for reform. Additionally, it examines the role of legislation and government intervention in addressing social and economic issues during this period.

Challenges to Industrialization

1. Exploitative Labor Practices: One of the most significant challenges to industrialization was the exploitation of labor, as workers faced long hours, low wages, and harsh working conditions in factories, mines, and mills. The rise of industrial capitalism led to the emergence of a working class that was subjected to unsafe working conditions, inadequate wages, and limited rights and protections.

2. Social Inequalities: The rapid economic growth and wealth accumulation of the Industrial Revolution exacerbated social inequalities, as industrialists and entrepreneurs amassed vast fortunes while workers struggled to make ends meet. The gap between the rich and the poor widened, leading to social unrest and discontent among the working class.

3. Environmental Degradation: Industrialization also brought about environmental degradation, as factories, mines, and mills polluted the air, water, and soil with toxic chemicals and pollutants. Deforestation, pollution, and resource depletion threatened the health and well-being of communities and ecosystems, raising concerns about the long-term sustainability of industrial development.

Labor Strikes, Protests, and Movements for

Reform

1. Labor Strikes and Protests: Workers responded to the challenges of industrialization through labor strikes, protests, and collective action. Throughout the 19th and early 20th centuries, labor unions organized strikes and protests to demand better wages, working conditions, and rights for workers. Strikes such as the Pullman Strike of 1894 and the Homestead Strike of 1892 highlighted the struggles of workers against exploitative labor practices and corporate power.

2. Social Movements for Reform: Social movements for reform emerged in response to the social and economic injustices of industrialization, advocating for political, social, and economic change. The labor movement, the women's suffrage movement, and the civil rights movement were among the many movements that fought for equality, justice, and democracy during this period. These movements mobilized activists, organizers, and ordinary citizens to demand reforms such as the eight-hour workday, child labor laws, and the right to vote.

3. Political Activism: Political activism played a crucial role in advancing social and economic reforms during the Industrial Revolution. Progressive politicians and reformers pushed for legislation to address the social and economic challenges of industrialization, leading to the passage of landmark laws such as the Fair Labor Standards Act, the Social Security Act, and the National Labor Relations Act. These laws provided protections and benefits for workers, established standards for wages and working conditions, and promoted social welfare and economic security.

Legislation and Government Intervention

1. Regulation of Industry: The government intervened in response to social and economic issues during the Industrial Revolution by enacting legislation to regulate industry and protect workers' rights. Laws such as the Factory Acts in Britain and the Fair Labor Standards Act in the

United States established standards for working conditions, hours of work, and child labor, aiming to improve the lives of workers and mitigate the worst abuses of industrial capitalism.

2. Creation of Social Programs: Government intervention also took the form of social programs and welfare policies designed to address poverty, unemployment, and social inequality. The establishment of social security systems, unemployment insurance, and public assistance programs provided economic support and assistance to individuals and families in need, promoting social welfare and economic security.

3. Investment in Infrastructure: Government investment in infrastructure played a crucial role in promoting economic development and expansion during the Industrial Revolution. Infrastructure projects such as the construction of canals, railroads, and highways facilitated the movement of goods, people, and capital, enabling the growth of industries and the expansion of markets. Government funding and support for infrastructure projects helped stimulate economic growth and create jobs, laying the groundwork for future prosperity.

In summary, resistance and reform were central features of the Industrial Revolution, as workers, activists, and politicians fought to address the social and economic challenges of industrialization. Labor strikes, protests, and social movements for reform pushed for better wages, working conditions, and rights for workers, while legislation and government intervention sought to regulate industry, protect workers' rights, and promote social welfare and economic security. Despite the challenges and obstacles they faced, the efforts of reformers and activists during the Industrial Revolution laid the groundwork for the social and economic progress that followed, shaping the world we inhabit today.

Chapter 14: Legacy of the Industrial Revolution

The Industrial Revolution left an indelible mark on American economy and society, shaping the course of history and laying the groundwork for the modern world. This chapter explores the enduring impact of the Industrial Revolution on the American economy and society, lessons learned, ongoing debates about industrialization, and its influence on subsequent technological revolutions and economic developments.

Enduring Impact on American Economy and Society

1. Economic Transformation: The Industrial Revolution transformed the American economy from agrarian-based to industrial powerhouse, fueling unprecedented economic growth, innovation, and prosperity. The rise of factories, mills, and industries revolutionized production processes, leading to increased productivity, efficiency, and wealth creation. Industrialization also spurred urbanization, as people migrated from rural areas to cities in search of employment and opportunity, leading to the growth of urban centers and the emergence of new social and cultural dynamics.

2. Social Transformation: The Industrial Revolution brought about profound social transformations, reshaping existing social structures and hierarchies. The rise of industrial capitalism led to the emergence of a new working class, composed of men, women, and children who labored in factories, mines, and mills under harsh conditions. Social inequalities widened, as industrialists and entrepreneurs amassed vast fortunes while workers struggled to make ends meet. However, the Industrial Revolution also provided opportunities for social mobility, enabling individuals to rise above their social origins through hard work, entrepreneurship, and innovation.

3. Technological Innovation: The technological innovations of the Industrial Revolution laid the groundwork for subsequent advancements in science, technology, and industry. Inventions such as the steam engine, cotton gin, and telegraph revolutionized transportation, communication, and manufacturing, paving the way for the development of new industries and technologies. The Industrial Revolution also sparked innovations in engineering, chemistry, and medicine, leading to breakthroughs such as the electric light bulb, the telephone, and the germ theory of disease.

Lessons Learned and Ongoing Debates about Industrialization

1. Environmental Impact: One of the key lessons learned from the Industrial Revolution is the importance of environmental stewardship and sustainability. The environmental consequences of industrialization, including pollution, deforestation, and resource depletion, highlight the need for responsible management of natural resources and ecosystems. Ongoing debates about industrialization center on balancing economic development with environmental protection, promoting sustainable growth, and mitigating the impacts of human activity on the planet.

2. Social Justice: The Industrial Revolution raised important questions about social justice, inequality, and labor rights that continue to resonate today. The struggles of workers for fair wages, safe working conditions, and basic rights during the Industrial Revolution highlight the need for social justice and economic equality. Ongoing debates about industrialization focus on addressing social inequalities, promoting inclusive growth, and ensuring that the benefits of economic development are shared equitably among all members of society.

3. Globalization: The Industrial Revolution ushered in an era of globalization, as goods, capital, and ideas flowed freely across national borders. The expansion of American industry and influence beyond

national borders reshaped global trade networks, geopolitics, and international relations. Ongoing debates about industrialization and globalization center on issues such as trade policy, economic integration, and the impact of global capitalism on developing countries and marginalized communities.

Influence on Subsequent Technological Revolutions and Economic Developments

1. Technological Revolutions: The Industrial Revolution laid the foundation for subsequent technological revolutions, including the Information Age, the Digital Revolution, and the Fourth Industrial Revolution. The advancements in science, technology, and industry during the Industrial Revolution set the stage for innovations such as the computer, the internet, and artificial intelligence, transforming the way we live, work, and communicate. The lessons learned from the Industrial Revolution continue to inform efforts to harness the power of technology for the benefit of humanity and address the challenges of the future.

2. Economic Developments: The Industrial Revolution paved the way for subsequent waves of economic development and growth, shaping the trajectory of capitalism and the global economy. The expansion of industries, markets, and trade networks during the Industrial Revolution laid the groundwork for the rise of modern capitalism and the emergence of the global economy. The lessons learned from the Industrial Revolution continue to inform efforts to promote sustainable economic development, foster innovation and entrepreneurship, and create opportunities for prosperity and growth.

3. Social and Cultural Dynamics: The Industrial Revolution had a profound impact on social and cultural dynamics, shaping the values, beliefs, and behaviors of individuals and societies. The rise of industrial capitalism and urbanization led to changes in family life, gender roles,

and social norms, as people adapted to the rhythms and realities of modern industrial society. The lessons learned from the Industrial Revolution continue to inform efforts to promote social cohesion, cultural diversity, and human flourishing in an increasingly interconnected and rapidly changing world.

In summary, the Industrial Revolution left a lasting legacy on American economy and society, shaping the course of history and influencing subsequent technological revolutions and economic developments. The lessons learned from the Industrial Revolution continue to inform ongoing debates about industrialization, globalization, and social justice, as we strive to build a more equitable, sustainable, and prosperous future for all.

Chapter 15: Reflections on the Future

As we stand at the threshold of the 21st century, the legacy of the Industrial Revolution continues to shape the trajectory of human civilization. This chapter reflects on the contemporary relevance of the Industrial Revolution, examines the challenges and opportunities in the 21st-century economy, and explores prospects for sustainable development and technological innovation in the future.

Contemporary Relevance of the Industrial Revolution

1. Technological Advancements: The Industrial Revolution set the stage for subsequent waves of technological innovation and progress, shaping the way we live, work, and communicate in the modern world. The advancements in science, technology, and industry during the Industrial Revolution laid the foundation for innovations such as the computer, the internet, and artificial intelligence, transforming every aspect of human society and ushering in the Digital Age.

2. Globalization and Interconnectedness: The expansion of American industry and influence beyond national borders during the Industrial Revolution laid the groundwork for the emergence of the global economy and the interconnected world we inhabit today. The lessons learned from the Industrial Revolution continue to inform efforts to promote economic integration, cultural exchange, and cooperation among nations in an increasingly interconnected and interdependent world.

3. Environmental Awareness and Sustainability: The environmental consequences of industrialization highlighted the need for responsible stewardship of natural resources and ecosystems, inspiring efforts to promote sustainability and environmental conservation in the 21st century. The lessons learned from the Industrial Revolution continue

to inform efforts to address climate change, pollution, and resource depletion, as we strive to build a more sustainable and resilient future for generations to come.

Challenges and Opportunities in the 21st Century Economy

1. Technological Disruption: The rapid pace of technological innovation and automation presents both challenges and opportunities in the 21st-century economy. While advancements in artificial intelligence, robotics, and biotechnology hold the promise of greater efficiency, productivity, and prosperity, they also raise concerns about job displacement, income inequality, and social disruption. Efforts to navigate the challenges of technological disruption and harness the opportunities for innovation and growth will be critical in shaping the future of work and economic development.

2. Globalization and Economic Integration: The forces of globalization and economic integration continue to reshape the global economy, creating new opportunities for trade, investment, and collaboration among nations. However, globalization also raises questions about inequality, environmental degradation, and social justice, as the benefits of economic growth and development are not always shared equitably among all members of society. Efforts to promote inclusive growth, sustainable development, and social cohesion in the face of globalization will be essential in addressing these challenges.

3. Environmental Sustainability: The imperative to address climate change, pollution, and resource depletion has become increasingly urgent in the 21st century, as the consequences of environmental degradation become more apparent. Efforts to promote environmental sustainability and conservation will require bold action, innovation, and collaboration across sectors and disciplines. From transitioning to

renewable energy sources to implementing sustainable agriculture practices, there are many opportunities to build a more sustainable and resilient future for the planet.

Prospects for Sustainable Development and Technological Innovation in the Future

1. Renewable Energy and Clean Technologies: The transition to renewable energy sources such as solar, wind, and hydroelectric power holds immense potential for addressing climate change and promoting sustainable development in the 21st century. Advances in clean technologies such as energy storage, electric vehicles, and smart grids are driving down costs and increasing efficiency, making renewable energy more accessible and affordable than ever before.

2. Digital Transformation and Connectivity: The digital transformation of the global economy is opening up new opportunities for innovation, entrepreneurship, and economic growth in the 21st century. The proliferation of digital technologies such as the internet of things, artificial intelligence, and blockchain is revolutionizing every sector of the economy, from healthcare and education to finance and manufacturing. Efforts to harness the power of digital technology for the benefit of humanity will be crucial in shaping the future of the digital economy.

3. Global Collaboration and Partnerships: Addressing the complex challenges of the 21st century will require global collaboration and partnerships across sectors, disciplines, and borders. From combating climate change and promoting sustainable development to addressing global health crises and advancing human rights, there are many opportunities for cooperation and collaboration in the pursuit of common goals. Efforts to build bridges, foster dialogue, and forge alliances will be essential in overcoming the challenges of the future and building a more prosperous, equitable, and sustainable world for all.

In conclusion, the Industrial Revolution continues to exert a profound influence on the trajectory of human civilization, shaping the way we live, work, and interact in the modern world. As we reflect on the lessons learned from the Industrial Revolution and look to the future, we are confronted with both challenges and opportunities in the 21st-century economy. By embracing innovation, sustainability, and collaboration, we can build a brighter future for generations to come, grounded in the enduring values of progress, prosperity, and human dignity.

Don't miss out!

Visit the website below and you can sign up to receive emails whenever Michael Johnson publishes a new book. There's no charge and no obligation.

https://books2read.com/r/B-A-OREFB-UAYAD

BOOKS 2 READ

Connecting independent readers to independent writers.

Did you love *The Industrial Revolution*? Then you should read *The Obama Presidency*[1] by Michael Johnson!

THE OBAMA PRESIDENCY

2

"Delve into the transformative era of 'The Obama Presidency: Hope and Change in the 21st Century.' From the historic campaign trail to the challenges of governing, this book offers an intimate look at Barack Obama's presidency. Explore key moments, from the passage of the Affordable Care Act to foreign policy crises and efforts to combat climate change. Reflect on Obama's legacy and the enduring impact of his presidency on American politics and society. A compelling narrative of hope, progress, and the complexities of leadership in the modern age."

---

1. https://books2read.com/u/boMWA9

2. https://books2read.com/u/boMWA9

About the Author

Michael Johnson is a distinguished historian specializing in American history. With a degree in History from Harvard University, Johnson's work delves into pivotal moments, figures, and themes shaping the United States. He has authored numerous acclaimed books, offering insightful perspectives and engaging narratives. Johnson's commitment to meticulous scholarship and compelling storytelling has earned him widespread acclaim in the field. Passionate about sharing his expertise, he frequently engages in lectures and public events to foster a deeper appreciation for America's past.